# VICTORY OVER GRIEF & SORROW

"SURELY HE HATH BORNE OUR GRIEFS,
AND CARRIED OUR SORROWS" • ISAIAH 53:4

DUFRESNE MINISTRIES
PUBLICATIONS

*Victory Over Grief & Sorrow*
ISBN: 978-0-940763-42-5
Copyright © 2018 by Dufresne Ministries

Published by:
Dufresne Ministries Publications
P.O. Box 1010
Murrieta, CA 92564
www.dufresneministries.org

1-2500

Unless otherwise indicated, all Scriptural quotations are from the *King James Version* of the Bible.

Scripture quotations marked *Amplified* are taken from the *Amplified Bible,* Copyright © 1954, 1958, 1962, 1964, 1965, 1987 by The Lockman Foundation. Used by permission.

Printed in the United States of America. All rights reserved under International Copyright Law. Contents and/or cover may not be reproduced in whole or in part in any form without the express consent of the publisher.

Cover design: Nancy Dufresne & Grant Dufresne

Cover Photo: Grant Dufresne © Dufresne Ministries Publications

# WORLD HARVEST
## BIBLE TRAINING CENTER
### MURRIETA · CALIFORNIA

TRAINING BELIEVERS TO MOVE WITH THE WORD & THE SPIRIT

---

FOR MORE INFO OR TO SUBMIT AN APPLICATION ONLINE, GO TO

## DUFRESNEMINISTRIES.ORG/whatiswhbtc

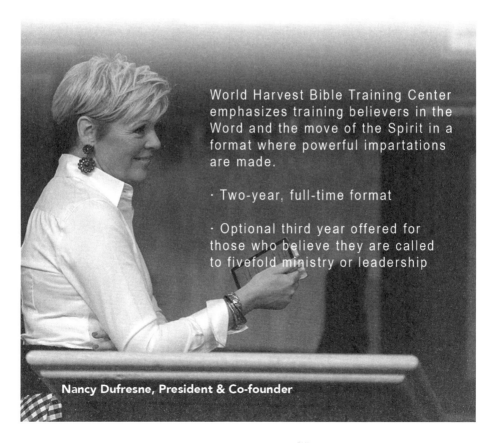

World Harvest Bible Training Center emphasizes training believers in the Word and the move of the Spirit in a format where powerful impartations are made.

- Two-year, full-time format

- Optional third year offered for those who believe they are called to fivefold ministry or leadership

**Nancy Dufresne, President & Co-founder**

# Books by Nancy Dufresne

*Daily Healing Bread from God's Table*

*His Presence Shall be My Dwelling Place*

*Victory in the Name*

*There Came a Sound From Heaven:
The Life Story of Dr. Ed Dufresne*

*The Healer Divine*

*Visitations from God*

*Responding to the Holy Spirit*

*God: The Revealer of Secrets*

*A Supernatural Prayer Life*

*Causes*

*I Have a Supply*

*Fit for the Master's Use:
A Handbook for Raising Godly Children*

*A Sound, Disciplined Mind*

*Knowing Your Measure of Faith*

*The Greatness of God's Power*

*Peace: Living Free from Worry*

*Following the Holy Spirit*

*An Apostle of the Anointing:
A Biography of Dr. Ed Dufresne*

# Contents

Introduction .................................................................. ix

1. The Force of Peace ............................................. 15
2. Redeemed from Grief & Sorrow ......................... 23
3. To Die is Gain ..................................................... 31
4. A Child in Heaven ............................................... 37
5. An Example for Others ...................................... 41
6. What's Your Attention On? ................................. 43
7. Two Kinds of Sorrow .......................................... 49
8. Light Afflictions .................................................. 55
9. Run Your Race with Joy ..................................... 65
10. A Husband to the Widow ................................... 71

*Prayer of Salvation* ............................................. 75

*How to be Filled with the Holy Spirit* ................. 77

*Prayer to Receive the Holy Spirit* ....................... 81

# Introduction

No matter what storms come to our lives, victory always belongs to God's people. There are many different kinds of storms that will offer us grief and sorrow, but when we know and believe what God's Word says, the door against grief and sorrow can be shut tight, forbidding their entrance into our lives.

Grief is not simply an emotion, but it is a destructive, evil force that will rob its victim of peace, joy, hope, faith, life, health, and soundness of mind. Jesus paid a great price for us to be redeemed from its life-stealing grip. He defeated this enemy for us, and we must take a firm stand of victory against it, knowing it is a defeated foe. It is not to be tolerated for a moment, but it is to be boldly stood against as a defeated, conquered enemy.

Grief is not to be considered an appropriate response to a test or difficulty. Contrary to what many think, it is not a way we express love, honor, and respect for someone who has passed away, but it is an enemy to mankind.

Isaiah 53:4 tells us, *"Surely he hath borne our griefs, and carried our sorrows...."* Something that cost Jesus so much is of immeasurable value to us – the price He paid and the victory He won for us means our complete and total freedom from the evil forces of grief and sorrow. Take your stand against them, refuse them, run them out of your life, and forbid their entrance by boldly declaring that Jesus has defeated grief and sorrow and has made you free from their power. Regardless of what you may feel, take your bold stand today and continually rejoice in your freedom from them.

Romans 15:4 tells us, *"For whatsoever things were written aforetime were written for our learning, that we through patience and COMFORT OF THE SCRIPTURES might have HOPE."* When we know what the Word says and believe it, we are comforted by the Word. The part of the Word we believe is the part that comforts us. The comfort the scriptures bring is unlike any human comfort that is offered us. But we must *allow* the scriptures to comfort us by believing and agreeing with them, and not rejecting the comfort they offer. We are to rest and recline ourselves upon them in faith, for the comfort they offer us is far greater than the discomfort of any test or storm. Hope is strong in those who will take the comfort the scriptures offer, and when hope is strong, the future is bright.

Luke 13:34 quotes Jesus, *"...How often I have desired and yearned to gather your children together [around Me], as a hen [gathers] her young under her wings, but YOU WOULD NOT!"* (Amplified) Jesus longed to bring help and comfort to His own people, but they wouldn't respond properly to Him.

To receive the comfort the scriptures offer us, we must respond rightly to them.

Hebrews 13:5 & 6 (Amplified) reads, *"...for He [God] Himself has said, I will not in any way fail you nor give you up nor leave you without support. [I will] not, [I will] not, [I will] not in any degree leave you helpless nor forsake nor let [you] down (relax My hold on you)! [Assuredly not!] So WE TAKE COMFORT and are encouraged and confidently and BOLDLY SAY, The Lord is my Helper; I will not be seized with alarm [I will not fear or dread or be terrified]...."*

How do the scriptures comfort us? How does the Lord help us? He gives us His Word to put in our mouths. As we boldly speak His Word and meditate upon it, guarding against and casting down any thoughts contrary to what He says in His Word, His comfort and help flow for us.

One of the greatest storms anyone can face is the death of a loved one, but even then, acting on and holding to God's Word will place you high above it all — high above circumstances, emotions, feelings, and fears. Your victory will not falter or slip at those times as God's Word is given its proper place. As you choose to act on and hold to His Word, you will enjoy the comfort, peace, joy, and victory His Word brings, and you will become an example to others of how great God's power is in the face of all enemies.

Wrong thinking is one thing that can open the door to grief and sorrow — not knowing that Jesus paid the price to redeem us from grief and sorrow, or people wrongly accusing God of either causing the death or not intervening to stop the death of a loved one.

No, God doesn't have anything to do with any tragedy or the death of a loved one, for John 10:10 tells us, *"The thief comes only in order to steal and kill and destroy. I came that they may have and enjoy life, and have it in abundance (to the full, till it overflows)"* (Amplified). So anything that steals, kills, and destroys comes from the enemy, not God. God is the life-giver, not the destroyer. God is a restorer.

The enemy delights when people mistake his actions as being God's actions, for then they will be subject to wrong thinking, which is the devil's point of entrance. When people think wrongly toward God concerning tragedy, then they fail to receive the fullness of comfort that the Word offers.

But when the Biblical truths and principles in this book are embraced, they will enable you to stand in your complete victory when faced with any storm, including the death of a loved one.

Don't allow any test, trial, or storm steal from you that comfort, peace, and joy that is yours. Draw on the Word and the greater One in you. Instead of taking what circumstances, the flesh, and this natural realm bring, take the comfort He offers.

> **1 THESSALONIANS 4:13-18** *(Amplified)*
> **13 Now also we would not have you ignorant, brethren, about those who fall asleep [in death], THAT YOU MAY NOT GRIEVE [FOR THEM] as the rest do who have no hope [beyond the grave].**
> **14 For since we believe that Jesus died and rose again, even so God will also bring with Him through Jesus those who have fallen asleep [in death].**
> **15 For this we declare to you by the Lord's [own] word, that we who are alive and remain until**

> **the coming of the Lord shall in no way precede [into His presence] or have any advantage at all over those who have previously fallen asleep [in Him in death].**
> **16 For the Lord Himself will descend from heaven with a loud cry of summons, with the shout of an archangel, and with the blast of the trumpet of God. And those who have departed this life in Christ will rise first.**
> **17 Then we, the living ones who remain [on the earth], shall simultaneously be caught up along with [the resurrected dead] in the clouds to meet the Lord in the air; and so always (through the eternity of the eternities) we shall be with the Lord!**
> **18 Therefore COMFORT AND ENCOURAGE ONE ANOTHER WITH THESE WORDS.**

These words are your comfort and encouragement as they are believed and held to. Take their comfort by meditating on them, speaking them, and focusing your attention on them. Don't exchange the comfort of these scriptures for any depression, grief, or sorrow that may be offered you.

The joy of life that God gives is so great that we are not to exchange any of that joy for the destructive forces of fear, depression, grief, or sorrow. Jesus paid such a great price to free us from them, for He doesn't want us to have one moment of interaction with them. He wants us to walk in total and complete freedom from them.

Hold to the Word and the hope His Word gives, for the future is bright!

## *Chapter 1*

# The Force of Peace

(It was on Friday, October 18, 2013, at about 10:30 am, that my oldest son, Stephen, his wife, Morgan, and my youngest son, Grant, filed out from the house to the back patio where I was sitting. I watched them as they came toward me, and I wondered why they had come to the house from the ministry offices. Morgan had a peculiar look on her face, and her eyes were glued on me.

Stephen was the first to speak. "Mom, Dad and Mitch (our pilot) were flying from Kansas this morning to Texas. About 20 minutes into the flight, their plane went down. There were no survivors." )

As I heard the words and began processing them, many things came to mind and fell into place. Over the previous six months, there had been many things that had come to me that I didn't understand, but with this news, they all fell into place.

In months past, as I would drive home from the offices, there were several different questions that would repeatedly come to me. Questions like, "How would you run the financial department? How would you run the publications department? What changes would you make if you were responsible for them?" Many like questions would come to me on different occasions. I would immediately dismiss any such thoughts. "Oh, no, I won't think like that. I refuse to entertain anything like that," I would say to myself.

But as Stephen broke the news to me, all those questions that had come to me suddenly made sense. God was preparing me for the position I would be unexpectedly thrust into.

Not only did those questions that had repeatedly come to me now make sense, but there had been many spiritual experiences that had taken place over the previous four years that had all played a role in preparing me for the news I was hearing. Prayer burdens, things God had said to me, instructions given by the Spirit, and various leadings by the Spirit over the past four years now made complete sense to me.

## The Comforter

One of the greatest roles the Holy Spirit plays in the life of the believer is that of Comforter, and one of the ways He comforts us is by preparing us. In the previous four years, He had been preparing me for this time.

No, it wasn't God's plan or His doing that this tragedy had occurred, but because He knew it was coming, He had prepared me so that this tragedy didn't take me, my family, the church family, or the ministry off course.

## Practicing Peace

I so clearly remembered two years prior, in 2011, the Spirit of God spoke to me and said, "All I want you doing is practicing peace." I knew what He meant by that. I was to guard my mind against any worrisome, troubling, disturbing, unsettling, fearful, or doubtful thoughts, refusing to entertain them in my thought life.

Kenneth E. Hagin, who was our spiritual father, had often said in his services, "How do you know if you're worrying? If you're thinking about it!" He taught us the importance of not worrying and of casting our cares on God if our faith was going to work. Worry and faith can't flow together.

In 2009, there was a season of testing that began for me, and it lasted for about one and a half years. During that time, there was a bombardment on my mind, and I had stood in faith against those tests. So, when the Spirit of God said to me, "All I want you doing is practicing peace," that was an instruction and a help that He gave me to pass through that season of testing.

Notice the phrase "practicing peace." Peace has to be practiced. No one gets good at anything without practice. That's true for natural things, but it's also true for spiritual things. Peace is a spiritual force and a flow that must be practiced.

When the Spirit said to me, "All I want you doing is practicing peace," He was not only giving me my answer for exiting that test I had faced for one and a half years, but He was also giving me my answer and help for this tragedy I would face two years later.

I had been faithful to do as the Spirit had instructed me. I diligently gave attention to practicing peace. Every thought that didn't lead me to peace, I immediately rejected and cast down. I didn't try to "get rid of wrong thoughts," for you can't keep wrong thoughts from coming, but you can keep from turning them over and over in your thought life – you can keep from entertaining them. When troubling thoughts would come, I would *answer them* with the Word, then ignore them and turn my attention to worshipping God. As I diligently did this, each troubling, worrisome thought was successfully overcome. I was consistently doing what Paul spoke in 2 Corinthians 10:5, *"CASTING DOWN imaginations, and every high thing that exalteth itself against the knowledge of God, and bringing into captivity EVERY thought to the obedience of Christ."*

No one can leave their mind unguarded and expect to live a life of peace. Peter instructed us, *"...gird up the loins of your mind..."* (1 Peter 1:13). That means to take control of your thought life, to discipline and guard your mind.

## A Sound Mind

Every thought that comes to your mind doesn't originate with your mind. The devil will certainly suggest troubling thoughts to your mind, and you can't stop him from doing that, but you can certainly refuse to entertain what he suggests and refuse to be troubled by those thoughts.

As Dad Hagin would often say, "You can't stop the birds from flying around your head, but you can certainly stop them from building a nest in your hair."

Part of the inheritance Jesus provided for us and that belongs to us is a sound mind. You are authorized to cast down every troubling thought and draw instead on the peace Jesus left you as your divine inheritance. Jesus told us, *"Peace I leave with you, my peace I give unto you..."* (John 14:27). The same peace that He operated in and that governed Him, He left with us. In the rest of this verse, He tells us what we must do if we're to experience and enjoy the peace He left us, *"...Let not your heart be troubled, neither let it be afraid."*

Yes, troubling and fearful thoughts and circumstances will come, but we are not to let them trouble us or make us afraid. We are to draw on the peace He left us instead of on the trouble and fear offered us. How do we draw on that peace? By turning our attention toward God through worshipping Him, and toward the words He has spoken.

## The Power of Suggestion

Colossians 2:15 tells us that Jesus, *"...having spoiled* (defeated, reduced to nothing, stripped) *principalities and powers, he made a show of them openly, triumphing over them in it."*

Jesus defeated and stripped Satan of his power to harm those who belong to God. The only power Satan has left is the power of suggestion. He will suggest troubling, fearful, doubtful, worrisome thoughts, and if people believe them, then he will trouble them. Don't believe them! Don't believe any thought, any condition, any circumstance more than you believe what God says.

### Peace – "In The Spirit"

For two years prior to this tragedy, I had diligently practiced peace, and I ended up in a flow of peace I had never experienced before. Really, walking in peace is a flow of walking in the Spirit. To walk in peace, you have to choose to live more aware of the spirit realm than the natural realm. Paul tells us, *"For to be carnally minded* (to be occupied with the natural realm) *is death; but to be spiritually minded* (to hold your attention on the things of God) *is life and PEACE"* (Rom. 8:6).

To be occupied with all that's going on in the natural realm will open the door for death to work. But to be occupied with and give attention to the things of God will open the door for life and peace to flow and dominate you.

When you live spiritually minded, the flow of peace will be so great that you will live days of Heaven on the earth (Deut. 11:21).

From emphasizing peace for two years prior to this tragedy, I was acquainted with and becoming more skillful at staying in that flow.

I had become more skillful at staying out of the mental arena so that I could stay in the spirit arena, the faith arena.

The devil works to draw us into the mental arena through the troubling thoughts he suggests, and if he can hold you in the mental arena, he'll defeat you, for that's his arena. The mental arena is the carnal arena. But if you will refuse to be drawn by his strategies into the mental arena, and stay in the spirit arena (the faith arena), then you'll overcome him.

You stay in the spirit arena by answering every wrong, troubling thought with the Word, and then turning your attention on God through worshipping and praising Him.

### The Fruit Of Peace

Galatians 5:22 & 23 tells us, *"But the fruit of the spirit* (the human spirit, not the Holy Spirit) *is love, joy, PEACE, longsuffering, gentleness, goodness, faith, meekness, temperance...."*

Peace is a fruit imparted by the Holy Spirit that is present in the spirit of every child of God. Fruit grows. Just as fruit on a tree grows, these fruits in your spirit need to grow. The more you water them with the Word, yield to them, and draw on them, the more they will grow, and the more they grow, the sweeter your life will be.

For two years, I had focused on developing this fruit of peace by feeding and acting on the Word, and by yielding to it. It moved my life into a place of great sweetness. As this fruit of peace grew, it became a great force that even death couldn't disturb or overcome. The power of death stood weak in the presence of this mighty force of peace.

## Chapter 2

# Redeemed from Grief & Sorrow

When my son told me of my husband's homegoing, I immediately warned my kids, "Don't you touch this in your thought life! Don't start asking questions like, 'Why did this happen?'"

Questions are of the mental arena. When you get into the arena of questions, you have just stepped into the mental arena. Stay in the spirit arena, which is the faith arena. There are no questions in the spirit arena – only answers. To get into the mental arena is to get entrenched in questions, but to stay in the spirit arena is to stay in the place where answers are.

I knew if the kids or I got into the mental arena, we would open the door to the devil to bring grief, sorrow, and depression, and that's why I warned them against getting into the mental arena. I told them, "If you get into the mental arena, you can get into a hole of depression. If you get into that hole, you're going to have to get back out of there. I don't have time to pull you or me out of that hole, so just don't ever go there!"

My kids and I sat on the back porch for about an hour or so and discussed the future and where we would go from there.

I thought to myself, "What was the last sermon I preached? My help and answers are in that sermon, because I know that God is in front of situations, not behind them, so He puts me in front of them, too."

On that Friday morning, I thought back to my last sermon in the midweek service at our church. I had preached on, "God Puts Your Answer In You Before Your Need Shows Up."

So I rested back on the awareness that none of this had caught God by surprise and that He had already stocked the shelves of my heart with all the answers that I would need for this situation. So, my job was to turn to my spirit and draw on and yield to those answers in me, rather than turning to the mental arena to search for answers there. The answers for our lives are in our spirits, not in our minds. Don't look in the wrong place for your answers.

Stephen had asked me, "Mom, what are we going to do now?"

I replied, "We are going to keep doing what we were already doing! Nothing changes! The church continues, the Bible school continues, the traveling ministry continues, and all other arms of the ministry continue."

I knew that although Ed had left this planet, the plan of God didn't leave with him – the plan was still fully intact.

My husband had poured so much into me and my children that we were prepared to keep moving forward. Never quit moving forward! Don't allow the devil to back you up one inch!

I didn't allow my mind to touch into thoughts like, "What about the house payments? What about the income of the ministry? How will this affect the church? What's going to happen to me in the future?" I didn't allow myself to go there. I knew if I stayed out of the mental arena and in the spirit arena, the answers that I needed would all come. I refused to leave peace. My help was in peace, not in worry.

## No Grief & Sorrow

The rest of that day was full of staff meetings, news reporters, and many incoming and outgoing phone calls. There were now two memorial services to plan, and every moment was full, planning and delegating all of the details and activities. Several of the staff members and Bible school students set up their computers and equipment on my kitchen table and counters as we planned and mapped out the days ahead. For the next 13 days and nights, there was little sleep for anyone. Some of the staff members would work nearly all night, catch a few winks of sleep on the couches, and then get up early and start again.

All the while, the peace of God was so tangible and precious to our family.

Early the next morning after Ed's homegoing, Grant, our 19-year-old son, brought me a letter he had written to his dad the night before. He expressed his love and honor for his dad. The peace of God was so evident upon him.

As I was up early to dress and start tending to the work and planning that needed to be done, I stood in the bathroom voicing my thoughts to God. "Father, I so appreciate and value the tangibility of Your peace upon me. But as the days pass, the tangibility of Your peace may not be as evident then. In the coming days, am I going to have a fight on my hands?" I had never had a really close loved one die before, so I was completely unsure of what to expect.

As I posed my question to God, I wanted to prepare myself for any mental opposition I might face. But as soon as I asked God my question, Jesus spoke to me. "I not only bore your sicknesses and pains, but I also bore your griefs and sorrows." When He said that, I knew I wouldn't have to deal with grief and sorrow in the coming days. I was redeemed from it, and as long as I continued to yield to and draw on the peace of God, that peace would mount guard over my heart and mind and protect me from any grief and sorrow.

> **ISAIAH 53:4 & 5** *(Amplified)*
> **4  Surely He has borne our GRIEFS (sicknesses, weaknesses, and distresses) and carried our SORROWS and pains [of punishment], yet we [ignorantly] considered Him stricken, smitten, and afflicted by God.**
> **5  But He was wounded for our transgressions, He was bruised for our guilt and iniquities; the chastisement [needful to obtain] PEACE AND WELL-BEING FOR US was upon Him, and with**

the stripes [that wounded] Him we are healed and made whole.

**PHILIPPIANS 4:6-9** *(Amplified)*
**6 Do not fret or have any anxiety about anything, but in every circumstance and in everything, by prayer and petition (definite requests), with thanksgiving, continue to make your wants known to God.
7 And GOD'S PEACE [SHALL BE YOURS... THAT PEACE] WHICH TRANSCENDS ALL UNDERSTANDING SHALL GARRISON AND MOUNT GUARD OVER YOUR HEARTS AND MINDS IN CHRIST JESUS.
8 For the rest, brethren, whatever is true, whatever is worthy of reverence and is honorable and seemly, whatever is just, whatever is pure, whatever is lovely and lovable, whatever is kind and winsome and gracious, if there is any virtue and excellence, if there is anything worthy of praise, think on and weigh and take account of these things [fix your minds on them].
9 Practice what you have learned and received and heard and seen in me, and model your way of living on it, and the God of peace (of untroubled, undisturbed well-being) will be with you.**

Although we are redeemed from grief and sorrow, the way to keep the door closed to it is to do what the verses listed above instruct – do not fret or have any anxiety about anything – refuse to worry about anything. How do you know if you're worrying? If you're thinking about it. Refuse to entertain thoughts of worry. Instead, yield to and draw on the peace that He has made yours. And as verse 8 instructs, only allow your mind to think on the right things.

## God's Presence

For several weeks after Ed's homegoing, all throughout each day, weepings would rise up. Thankfully, I recognized what those weepings were. When the presence of God is strong upon you, you'll weep. His presence was coming upon me at different times throughout those weeks to comfort me.

God's presence will come upon His people to comfort them at times of difficulty. If people don't recognize those weepings as His presence that comes to comfort, they will process those weepings mentally and associate them with the difficulty they are facing, and they will go into the emotional arena and start processing what they're facing through their emotions. If they do that, the devil will take advantage of them getting in that emotional arena, and grief and sorrow will try to get in.

If those weepings come, learn to recognize that it's His presence that's coming to comfort you, and start worshipping Him. Turn your thoughts toward Him and away from any difficulties, and you will find that His presence and peace will hold you above any grief and sorrow.

I also instructed our congregation along these same lines, for I knew that just as God's presence would come to comfort me, He would also comfort them in the same way, and I wanted them to recognize how to respond properly to those weepings – with their spirits and not with their minds and emotions.

*Chapter 3*

# To Die is Gain

When you know and believe what the Word says about those who go home to be with the Lord, you don't respond the same way others respond. In fact, when Ed went home to be with the Lord, I knew too much to act like I didn't know it.

Paul stated in Philippians 1:21, *"...to live is Christ, and to die is GAIN."* When a Christian dies, they gain! We must believe it when the Word tells us that. To gain means that it's better there than here on earth.

For the believer, nothing ends at the grave. They just enter into greater glories and rewards – they gain! In fact, if given the opportunity, none of those who enter Heaven would choose to come back to Earth. They are not only in your past, but are also in your future, for you will have a glorious reunion with them one day.

When a loved one dies, you don't "lose them." You know right where they are. They are in Heaven – a place of "gain." Remember that and rejoice about it. It will keep the door closed to depression, grief, and sorrow.

If someone gained in the natural – got promoted on the job, moved into a bigger and better home, or received a large check – our response wouldn't be to grieve or sorrow. No, we would rejoice with them over their gain.

Well, when a Christian dies, they gain, and it's a far greater increase than anything naturally that could be gained. Therefore, our appropriate response should be to rejoice at their gain, not grieve.

I appreciate the story one woman tells about her own experience. Her husband had died in mid-life, and she had struggled with grief. After about one year of struggling, she asked Jesus a question. "Jesus, if You were me, what would You do differently than I am doing?" What a great question she asked.

He answered back, "I would quit focusing on what you lost and focus on what he gained." What an answer!

He pinpointed the door that grief comes through. When we focus on ourselves and on our loss, then depression, grief, and sorrow are the result. But when we consider our loved one's gain, there's no room for grief.

Many times, our tears are selfish tears, thinking of ourselves instead of thinking of what they gained.

Yes, I understand that when a loved one is no longer present here, there are adjustments to make regarding their absence, but the Holy Spirit will assist you with that if you will look to and yield to Him.

Remember, the plan of God for your life did not exit with a loved one; therefore, the greatness of God's plan for you is still intact, so there's much for you to rejoice about. Your future is bright.

**Grief is Not an Expression of Love**

Paul instructs us, *"But I would not have you to be ignorant, brethren, concerning them which are asleep, that ye SORROW NOT, even as others which have no hope"* (1 Thess. 4:13).

When you're not walking in ignorance, but are walking in the light, you see that you can choose to "sorrow not."

Some may think that grief and sorrow are appropriate when a loved one dies, but if we believe the Word, that they gained, then grief and sorrow aren't appropriate. Jesus paid the price so that we wouldn't have depression, grief, and sorrow.

Many think that grieving and being sorrowful is expressing love, respect, and honor for those who died, but grief and sorrow are not a flow of love. It is not a display of love, but rather, it's a part of the curse that Jesus redeemed us from.

Yes, many Christians will even think that something is wrong with you if you don't grieve and show sorrow for a loved one who died, but when you know and believe what the Word says, you're not obligated to respond like those who don't know the Word.

I know first-hand that the force of peace is FAR greater than death. Peace is not simply a feeling, but it's a force that makes you masterful in the face of death. It's a force that puts you on top when faced with great tragedy, crisis, and difficulty.

Believe the Word! Don't let the homegoing of a loved one cause you to cast your faith aside. That's when faith is needed the most, and when the force faith carries is most evident. Don't cast it aside; faith is for times of opposition.

For almost 30 years, I had been a student of my husband's life and ministry. I decided that I was going to show myself to have been a good student of what he had taught and poured into me for almost three decades. That's how I show honor and love for him, by doing what he taught me about the Word and about walking in faith, not by grieving and being sorrowful.

Smith Wigglesworth made the statement after his own wife went home to be with the Lord, "If you go on mourning the loss of loved ones who have gone to be with Christ, I say this in love to you, you have never had the revelation that Paul spoke of when he showed us it is better to go than to stay."

### Choose Life & Blessing

God tells us in Deuteronomy 30:19, *"...I have set before you life and death, blessing and cursing: therefore CHOOSE LIFE...."* When you chose to be born again, you made a choice for life. But now that you're born again, you still have choices to make. When you're faced with circumstances and difficulties, you have a choice to make – choose life. When you're faced with symptoms, choose to believe you're healed. When you're faced with lack, choose to believe prosperity is yours. When you're faced with fear, choose faith. When you're faced with grief and sorrow, choose peace and joy.

Nothing can take your choice from you. When the tragedy of my husband's premature death happened, that event didn't take my choice from me. I still had a choice of how I would respond to it. I could have chosen depression, grief, and sorrow, but I didn't – I chose peace, I chose to believe God's Word. I chose the blessing of peace, not the curse of grief and sorrow.

No matter what emergencies and difficulties arise in your life, you can still choose life and blessing. In Deuteronomy 30:19, God even gives you the answer – "choose life." That's always the right choice, for that's the choice that God tells you to make. Make sure you make the right choice, for your choice is your future!

### Choose God's Plan

When Ed went to Heaven, God's plan for my life didn't leave with him. God's plan for me was still intact, but I had to choose to continue on in His plan. I believed that nothing of His plan was lost to me.

People will enter your life, and people will exit your life. Realize that God's plan for your life doesn't exit with them. The future is still bright! God's plan for you is still full! God's plan is still yours for the choosing!

## *Chapter 4*

# A Child in Heaven

King David's first son with Bathsheba fell sick. For seven days, David had fasted and prayed for the child, but the child died. 2 Samuel 12:19-24 records it.

> **2 SAMUEL 12:19-24**
> 19 But when David saw that his servants whispered, David perceived that the child was dead: therefore David said unto his servants, Is the child dead? And they said, He is dead.
> 20 Then David arose from the earth, and washed, and anointed himself, and changed his apparel, and came into the house of the Lord, and worshipped: then he came to his own house; and when he required, they set bread before him, and he did eat.
> 21 Then said his servants unto him, What thing is this that thou hast done? thou didst fast and weep for the child, while it was alive; but when the child was dead, thou didst rise and eat bread.
> 22 And he said, While the child was yet alive, I fasted and wept: for I said, Who can tell whether God will be gracious to me, that the child may live?
> 23 But now he is dead, wherefore should I fast? can I bring him back again? I SHALL GO TO HIM, BUT HE SHALL NOT RETURN TO ME.

**24 And David comforted Bathsheba his wife, and went in unto her, and lay with her: and she bare a son, and he called his name Solomon: and the Lord loved him.**

## Resume Living

David gave us the example of how we are to respond to the death of a loved one, whether it's a child or an adult who lived out their life. Once the child died, David didn't linger in that situation. Instead, he resumed living. No amount of grief or sorrow would bring the child back. Grief and sorrow changes nothing for the better. It can't restore anything or anyone or bring comfort. It makes nothing better, but only serves to work further damage to its victims.

Don't allow the mind to touch on and linger on sorrowful thoughts, like what might have been. Instead, worship God for His great care for that one who is now in Heaven with Him.

David didn't yield to grief and sorrow, but instead encouraged himself in the truth that he would again see the child one day when he stated, *"I shall go to him, but he shall not return to me."* No, the child was not coming back, but that wasn't the end – David encouraged himself with the reminder, *"I shall go to him."*

God blessed David and restored to him what had been lost – He gave him another son, Solomon, who grew to be one of the great kings of history. That which the enemy meant to become a place of defeat, God turned to great restoration and blessing.

## A Child in Heaven

David knew he would again see his child in heaven. Every child who dies goes to heaven, whether they ever heard the salvation message or not, for they have not yet reached the age of accountability, therefore, they are not accountable for any sin or wrongdoing. But they will grow and come to full maturity in the abundant care of Heaven. So, you can rejoice greatly for God's great care for them. You are not the only one to love them, for He loved them first.

No, God doesn't have anything to do with the death of a child or of any loved one, for John 10:10 tells us that Satan is the one who steals, kills, and destroys. So anything that steals, kills, and destroys comes from the enemy, not God. God is the life-giver, not the destroyer. God is the One who provides great and everlasting care for them once they are in Heaven.

For the Christian, nothing ends at the grave; you will see that loved one again. They are now part of that great company of believers watching and cheering you on from the grandstands of Heaven. So, resume living! Don't linger in that situation. There's still much ahead for you. Carry on with God's plan for your life and in His great restoration power. There's still much to do. The future is bright!

*Chapter 5*

# An Example for Others

Realize that your choices affect other people. How you respond affects others.

My husband went home to be with the Lord on a Friday, and I knew that the Sunday morning service was especially important for our congregation and the direction the church would go. At that time, I had been their pastor for 22 years, setting an example for their own lives. Even though I was faced with this tragedy, I was still their pastor, and it was so important what example I set for them. I refused to allow a spirit of grief and sorrow to come into the church and upon the people. The momentum of faith and anointing in our church was too important to let grief and sorrow rob that momentum from us.

Those who served in the Ministry of Helps would arrive the earliest on Sunday morning, and I told my kids to be there to meet with them upon their arrival, and to let them know that our love and respect for Ed could not be demonstrated through grief and sorrow, but only through faith and rejoicing.

If my family would have demonstrated sorrow, then out of respect for us, the congregation would have responded the same way, but I wanted them to know that sorrow was not our response, so they were not obligated to respond with sorrow. But rather, they could take their cues from us.

My husband's life and ministry had brought so much blessing to them and to countless others, and that was to be their focus. They were not to focus on any loss, but rather on gratitude for all the gain and blessing he had brought to their lives and the lives of others.

Our congregation did take their cues from us, and we had a service of tremendous praise and rejoicing before God, and we closed tight the door against grief and sorrow.

Because the congregation followed us into greater places of faith, increase continued to flow and operate in the church, and God's plan has continued to flourish. The blessings of God upon us have been so apparent and rich, and none of God's plan has been lost.

The church family honored my husband in the greatest way possible – by holding fast to all of the Word that he had sowed into us – and that Word not only anchored us, but it promoted us during that time of testing.

Being a doer of the Word made all the difference.

## Chapter 6

# What's Your Attention On?

I remember an experience that I had years ago. I was out running errands one day when I got a phone call telling me that a woman who attended our Bible school had been killed in a car wreck.

Immediately, all kinds of thoughts sprang to mind. "How come I didn't perceive any danger for her? Have I not been praying enough? Why did I miss that?" All these questions began to fill my mind. They brought self-accusation and a sense of condemnation. Within moments, a tangible sense of grief tried to overwhelm me.

Just at that moment, Jesus asked me a question, "Where is she?"

"Well, she's in Heaven right now," I replied.

"Then can you not be thankful and joyful that she did not go to hell, but is rejoicing in Heaven right now?"

I did what He said and began to thank Him that she didn't go to hell, but went to Heaven because of the price that He paid for her. Within moments, all of the grief had left because I had shut the door to it through praising God and putting my attention on the right thing.

I saw that I had allowed my mind to go the wrong direction. Thinking negative thoughts, trying to figure out what I could have done to change this, and focusing on the fact that she was no longer on this earth were all thoughts that were going in the wrong direction.

You can't allow your mind and thought life to go in the wrong direction and think you're going to end up in the right place.

The mind allowed to go in the wrong direction will take a life in the wrong direction; it will open up a life to the wrong things of depression, grief, sorrow, and fear.

These things are not only bad, they are wrong for a believer. Jesus paid such a great price for us to be free from these tormenting things, and it's to our great benefit to discipline our thought lives so that we keep the door closed to these wrong things.

### Don't Give Place To The Devil

In Ephesians 4:27, Paul warns us, *"Neither give place to the devil."* The devil can't *take* a place in us, but we can sure *give* him a place in us.

One way we can give place to the devil is by not disciplining our thought lives. If we allow ourselves to become entrenched in the mental arena by asking and entertaining questions, by getting under a sense of guilt and condemnation, by dwelling on our loss, and by letting our emotions run unguarded, we will give place to the devil.

Anything that puts you down, accuses you, condemns you, or makes you fearful, worried, doubtful, or frustrated is from the enemy and is to be immediately rejected.

Some will even use these difficulties to gain sympathy from others, but all of these things, if not resisted, will open the door to depression, grief, and sorrow.

If you *gave* place to the devil, you can *take back* the place you gave him by resisting these things instead of yielding to them.

Jesus told us, *"Behold, I give unto YOU power* (authority) *to tread on serpents and scorpions, and over ALL the power of the enemy: and* (when you use your authority) *NOTHING shall by any means hurt you"* (Luke 10:19). When grief, sorrow, depression, fear, or anything else from the devil comes, talk to it. Use the authority Jesus gave you and tell these things to leave you! Don't wait for God to do something about them. Jesus gave *you* the authority, so you're the one who has to use your authority and run these things off, refusing to yield to them.

James told us, *"...Resist the devil, and he WILL flee from you"* (James 4:7). You resist these things that the devil brings by telling them to leave you in Jesus' Name!

What you don't resist will remain. Resist these things, and you're resisting the devil. Speak boldly to them and tell them to go! Refuse them!

Fight the good fight of faith! That's the only fight the believer is called on to engage in. The fight of faith is a fight of words. When wrong thoughts, accusations, and fearful, troublesome words come to you, answer them with the Word! Resist them and tell them to go from you in Jesus' Name!

Learn to recognize that not all thoughts that come to you originate with you. The devil will send thoughts to you, but recognize their origin and say, "That's not *my* thought! I refuse to take it in Jesus' Name!"

## A Sound Mind – Our Inheritance

*"For God hath not given us the spirit of fear; but of power, and of love, and of a SOUND MIND"* (2 Tim. 1:7).

Part of our inheritance that Jesus purchased for us is a sound mind. A sound mind is free from fear, worry, doubt, depression, anxiety, panic, and confusion. All of these are symptoms of and the offspring of fear. These things will come to all of us, but we don't have to let them in. Resist them!

We must discipline our thought lives to not allow our thoughts to just go in any direction they may want to go.

When you raise children, they must be disciplined so that their lives are kept safe and so they are a joy for others to be around.

Likewise, we must discipline our thought lives so that our own lives are kept safe, and so we are a joy to be around.

The Word has much to say about having a disciplined, sound thought life. Peter tells us, *"...gird up the loins of your mind..."* (1 Peter 1:13).

Paul instructs us, *"Casting down imaginations, and every high thing that exalteth itself against the knowledge of God, and bringing into captivity EVERY THOUGHT to the obedience of Christ"* (2 Cor. 10:5).

Learn to discipline your thought life on the everyday things so that when a test shows up, you'll already be skillful at holding your attention on the right thing.

*Chapter 7*

# Two Kinds of Sorrow

The Word speaks of two kinds of sorrow in 2 Corinthians 7:10.

    1) godly sorrow that leads to repentance

    2) worldly sorrow that worketh death

Worldly sorrow should not find any place in the believer, for that sorrow only steals from people and works death, not life, in them. No person's life ever became better as a result of worldly sorrow. Grief never elevated anyone's life. Depression never lifted anyone up. All of these things are worldly sorrow at work.

Godly sorrow is the only sorrow that a Christian is to have any experience with. If we miss God, if we commit sin and miss the mark, then godly sorrow will bring us to a place of repentance. When we repent, God forgives us and cleanses us from all unrighteousness (1 John 1:9). Therefore, this godly sorrow works to lift us, not bury us in a hole of depression and grief, like worldly sorrow does.

Paul told us in 1 Thessalonians 4:13 that we are not to sorrow, as others which have no hope.

A Christian is not like the rest of the world. We have hope! To sorrow with worldly sorrow is inappropriate for us – it doesn't fit us. Those in the world have no peace, they have no joy – but we do! Their only happiness is in people, places, or things, so if any of those vary, their happiness is affected. Our great joy is in the Lord Himself, so no matter who may enter or exit our lives, no matter what things may change around us, our joy remains the same, for Jesus is the source of our great joy! Because He is unchanging, our joy is unchanging.

## Spiritually Minded

We must renew our minds to enjoy this place of spirituality that belongs to us. To realize that Jesus is the fountain of all of our unshakeable joy takes a spiritual mindset.

Paul tells us, *"For to be carnally minded is death; but to be spiritually minded is LIFE and PEACE"* (Rom. 8:6). So, does it matter what your mindset is at a time of testing? Absolutely! Does it matter what you allow yourself to think on? Absolutely! One mindset is peace and life, the other is death. What you put your mind on is life or death to you.

If you're going to have a carnal mindset, allowing yourself to think like and respond like the rest of the world, it will work the death flow of this world in you. The carnal mind yields to fear, which will destroy faith. Grief, sorrow, and depression are all flows of death that Jesus has redeemed us from, and we must not allow them to have a place in us. If Christians have a carnal, natural, worldly mindset – thinking like the world, responding like the world who has no hope – that carnal mindset will open the door to the flow of death that's in the world.

But Christians are to be spiritually minded, which will bring us and anchor us into a flow of life and peace.

To be spiritually minded, we have to think on the Word, have our attention on the Word, and act in line with the Word. We are to refuse to allow any response that is like the world. We are to refuse to take our views and cues from a joyless, peaceless world.

### Don't Be Led by Emotions

To be spiritually minded is to stay in the arena of peace. But to leave the spirit arena and yield to emotions will open the door to grief and sorrow.

Emotions are part of the soulish arena of man. (Man is a threefold being. He is a spirit, he has a soul, which is made up of the mind, the will, and the emotions, and he lives in a body.) Although emotions are part of man's being, they are not to lead us.

Those who yield to and are led by their emotions will live unsteady and unstable lives because emotions will rise and fall at a whim. Someone's emotions can be up one minute and down the next. So leaning on or being led by your emotions will always leave you in a bad place.

Especially at a time of testing, tragedy, or difficulty, always keep your emotions in check, not letting them run off with you. Refuse to be led by them because they are a doorway through which grief, sorrow, and depression can enter.

Instead of being drawn into the soulish arena, where your emotions can dominate you, choose to stay in the spirit arena. One way you do that is by praising God, especially when your emotions try to lead you in a negative direction. Choose the flow of life and peace; choose to be spiritually minded.

## Attend To His Words

Proverbs 4:20-22 also tells us how to enjoy the flow of life that belongs to us.

> **20 My son, attend to** (put your attention on) **my words; incline thine ear unto my sayings.**
> **21 Let them not depart from thine eyes; keep them in the midst of thine heart.**
> **22 For they are life unto those that find them, and health to all their flesh.**

The flow of this world fights for our attention, but in these verses, God instructs us what to do with our attention – put it on His Word. We do that by turning our natural ears and the ears of our spirit toward what His Word says to us and away from all else, no matter how loudly other things clamor for our attention. But it doesn't stop there. Our eyes are involved in where our attention goes. We must choose to focus on His Word instead of on all that the opposition shows us. His words must also find their place in our hearts if they are going to produce life. Our ears, eyes, and hearts are to be absorbed with God's words so that our attention will stay anchored on His Word in a time of testing and opposition.

Where your attention goes, your faith goes. Make sure your attention and faith are firmly fixed on His Word, for it's the only thing great enough to deliver and protect you.

No casual, half-hearted attempt will do to fix your gaze on the right thing during a time of testing. You must give an all-out effort to His Word, and His power will meet you.

Choose the Word when something else is fighting for your attention, *for where your attention goes, your life goes!*

*Chapter 8*

# Light Afflictions

You have a race to run. God has a plan for your life that you're to fulfill. And you're not running this race alone — you're running in full view of those loved ones who have gone to Heaven before you. They are in the grandstands of Heaven cheering you on. They are so interested in you fulfilling God's plan for your life.

> **HEBREWS 12:1-3**
> **1 Wherefore seeing we also are compassed about with so great a cloud of witnesses, let us lay aside every weight, and the sin which doth so easily beset us, and let us run with patience the race that is set before us,**
> **2 Looking unto Jesus the author and finisher of our faith; who for the joy that was set before him endured the cross, despising the shame, and is set down at the right hand of the throne of God.**
> **3 For consider him that endured such contradiction of sinners against himself, lest ye be WEARIED and FAINT in your MINDS.**

Verse three tells us where quitting begins — when people get weary, they faint or quit in their minds. These verses tell us what to do so that we don't quit – consider Him. Consider what He did when He was faced with enduring the cross. Verse two tells us how He endured. *"...who for the JOY that was set before him endured the cross...."* How did He endure? He focused on the joy that was set before Him, which was on the other side of the cross. He looked clear through and past the cross, and He focused on the joy that was on the other side – the joy of being raised and seated at the right hand of the Father in total victory.

There's always "the other side" of every test. Don't get so focused on the test in front of you that you fail to see what awaits you on the other side of it. In fact, the way to endure and not faint in your mind is to look past the test you face and focus on the victory that awaits you. That's how Jesus endured. If you're to endure, that's what you must do, too.

## Paul's Victories

Paul faced great opposition, but he always endured. He tells some of the tests he faced. *"...in afflictions, in necessities, in distresses, in stripes, in imprisonments, in tumults, in labours, in watchings, in fastings"* (2 Cor. 6:4 & 5).

> **2 CORINTHIANS 11:23-27**
> **23 ...in stripes above measure, in prisons more frequent, in deaths oft.**
> **24 ...five times received I forty stripes save one.**
> **25 Thrice was I beaten with rods, once was I stoned, thrice I suffered shipwreck, a night and a day I have been in the deep;**

**26** In journeyings often, in perils of waters, in perils of robbers, in perils by mine own countrymen, in perils by the heathen, in perils in the city, in perils in the wilderness, in perils in the sea, in perils among false brethren;
**27** In weariness and painfulness, in watchings often, in hunger and thirst, in fastings often, in cold and nakedness.

**2 CORINTHIANS 4:8 & 9**
**8** We are troubled on every side, yet not distressed; we are perplexed, but not in despair;
**9** Persecuted, but not forsaken; cast down, but not destroyed.

## The Spirit Of Faith

This is an astounding list of oppositions and persecutions the apostle Paul faced! How did he endure so much? He tells us the answer just a few verses later in 2 Corinthians 4:13 & 14, *"We having the same SPIRIT OF FAITH, according as it is written, I believed, and therefore have I spoken; we also believe, and therefore speak; Knowing that he which raised up the Lord Jesus shall raise up us also by Jesus...."*

Paul endured because he had a spirit of faith. That spirit of faith caused him to speak the right thing in all his adversities. He believed that the God Who raised Jesus from the dead would also work in his behalf.

But some of Paul's most astounding statements about all of the persecutions that he faced were found just a few verses later in 2 Corinthians 4:17, *"For our LIGHT AFFLICTION,*

*WHICH IS BUT FOR A MOMENT, WORKETH FOR US a far more exceeding and eternal weight of glory."*

This is a tremendous statement! He calls all of his persecutions and oppositions a *light affliction* which was but for *a moment!* What kind of man was this, one who could call such great persecutions that would break most men a *light affliction?* He was a man with a spirit of faith!

### Opposition Works For You

Plus, Paul said that all of these afflictions were working *for him!* They worked for him because they put him in a position where only God could deliver him, and the glory of God was manifested in greater ways and did deliver him. He would never have experienced such displays of God's glory if he hadn't been in such places of opposition.

I understand in some small measure what Paul meant here. When my husband went home to be with the Lord, there were several large projects that Ed had in progress. He had been working for five years, trying to complete them. So, upon his death, I not only had to deal with his homegoing, but these projects had to be completed, as well, and I also became financially responsible for millions of dollars. There were huge pressing financial and business needs, including finishing construction on two buildings.

On every side, I was faced with looming responsibilities, as well as carrying on with the work of the ministry. But I refused to worry. I cast all my cares on Him, and He undertook for me. I did as Peter instructed, *"Casting the whole of your care [all your anxieties, all your worries, all your concerns, once and for all] on Him, for He cares for you affectionately and cares about you watchfully"* (1 Peter 5:7, Amplified). I knew that if I worried, that would be taking the cares out of His hands and into my own. If I did that, then He couldn't work for me. But as long as I refused to worry, I was leaving the cares in His hands so He could work on them.

I can say with Paul, that all of these responsibilities *worked for me!* I was in such a place of need, that God was the only One Who could have ever brought us to a place of completion on these things – and He did!

Within one year, all of the projects were fully completed! And I saw God's power manifest for us time and time again! God continually impressed me by His great working in our behalf. His power was displayed for us in mighty ways!

That which could have been a place of downfall and undoing was for us only a *light affliction!* It did not rob us of peace and joy. It didn't trouble or worry us. Every day, we would speak with a spirit of faith of the greatness of God's ability to work for us, and He surpassingly met our great expectation of Him!

Now, I know first-hand how Paul could call his persecutions a *light affliction.* The greatness of God's power makes all heavy things light!

Paul spoke of this in his prayers for the Ephesians, that they would know, *"...what is the exceeding greatness of his power to us-ward who believe…"* (Eph. 1:19). God's power is so great that it easily exceeds any and all other things that would work against us. And it goes into operation for *"…us-ward who believe…."*

What do those with the spirit of faith do? Paul told us in 2 Corinthians 4:13 – we believe, and therefore speak! Boldly say what God will do and is doing for you now! Focus on and put your attention on what God is doing *for* you, rather than looking at and focusing on what is coming *against* you!

### Light Affliction

How could Paul call all of his persecutions a light affliction? They were light compared to the glory and power of God that was working for him to deliver him.

He tells us the key to seeing all persecutions and tests as light. *"While we look not at the things which are seen, but at the things which are not seen: for the things which are seen are temporal; but the things which are not seen are eternal"* (2 Cor. 4:18).

Since God's Word instructs us not to focus on and put our attention on the natural, visible things, then it's a sin and wrong to focus there. God telling us not to focus on what we can see is for our own benefit, for faith won't work when we're focused on the wrong thing.

Don't focus on all of the difficulties and oppositions that are so visible, but instead, by faith you are to focus on what the natural eye can't see – the power, the glory, the anointing, the ability, and all of the grace and might of God that is available to you to work in your behalf. Focus on and put your attention on these things instead. As you do, and as you talk about these great forces that work for you, all things that try to work against you – all of the light afflictions – will be easily overcome by the greatness of God's power and glory that are working for you.

Every affliction and opposition is light compared to the weightiness of the glory that's working for you!

## For A Moment

I so love this statement that Paul made regarding his persecutions, *"For our light affliction, which is but FOR A MOMENT..."* (2 Cor. 4:17). Paul is telling us that there is to be a timeline on how long persecutions and difficulties are to affect us – for a moment! No longer! It only takes a moment for you to turn away from the opposition that can strike like a fiery dart, and instead, focus on and put your attention on the Word that is your victory. It only takes a moment to release your faith and enter into the peace and rest that faith gives.

Many are waiting for the devil to leave them alone and for opposition to stop so they can be peaceful. But faith doesn't wait for that! Faith learns to ignore and be unimpressed by arising opposition, because it is so attentive to and focused on what the Word says and on the power of God that's available to faith.

One of my favorite scriptures is Philippians 4:11, which Paul wrote from a Philippian prison, *"...FOR I HAVE LEARNED how to be content (satisfied to the point where I AM NOT DISTURBED OR DISQUIETED) in whatever state I am"* (Amplified).

This is the mastery of faith – where nothing troubles, unsettles, frightens, or disturbs you, for you have mastered holding your attention on God and His Word instead of on the opposition and the natural arena.

Paul wasn't waiting to get out of prison so he could be peaceful. Rather, he had learned to be completely untroubled and unaffected while he was sitting right in the middle of a wrong place. That's what the spirit of faith will do for you. It will hold you in total peace while you are completely surrounded by all that is wrong!

Psalm 23:5 tells us how this is possible, *"Thou preparest a table before me in the presence of mine enemies...."* No, the devil and opposition aren't going to leave you alone. They are present. But God tells you what to do right in their presence – eat of the great provision of His Word that He has spread before you. Make your enemies watch you eat your victory! Don't even give the enemies that are present a moment of your attention. Instead, occupy yourself with eating the truth of His Word. Give your full and total attention to the Word, not giving a moment's notice to the enemies that are present. The only thing your enemy is worthy of is of being ignored!

John tells us, *"...this is the victory that overcometh the world, even our faith"* (1 John 5:4). Your victory is waiting for your faith to show up! When you join your faith to God's Word, victory is the result.

When you add your faith to the Word of God, your affliction will only last a moment. Oh yes, the circumstances may last longer, but they won't affect you for more than a moment, for faith will move you into immediate victory.

Victory isn't yours only when the circumstances cease. Victory is yours the moment you attach your faith to the Word. Although circumstances may linger, you move immediately into victory with your faith, and the circumstances will always line up.

The mistake many make is that they allow that which opposes them to last longer than a moment. Some even allow it to last a lifetime! God's Word gives us the timeline on how long any opposition is to affect us – no longer than a moment!

Why does it last longer, and even a lifetime, for some? Because they hold their attention on what opposes them instead of on the Word. Where your attention goes, your faith goes.

Don't allow what's to only last for a moment last a lifetime!

Psalm 30:5 tells us that, *"...weeping may endure for A NIGHT, but joy cometh in the morning."* Even under the Old Testament, weeping wasn't to last more than a night – not many nights – but one night. Joy was to be the flow that followed the weeping. But in the New Testament, Paul stated that the timeline had been shortened from a night to a moment – for it only takes a moment to release your faith!

*Chapter 9*

# Run Your Race with Joy

No matter what has happened in your life, God still has a great plan for you to fulfill. Give yourself to living the life you were born for. Run your race! But it matters *how* you run – you are to run with joy!

It's a great privilege and an honor to run the race that God has for our lives, so we are to display great joy in having the wonderful privilege of running a race He authored for us. To run with less than joy is to dishonor and diminish the privilege of obeying Him in our race.

Remember, those who have gone before you and are watching from the grandstands of Heaven are interested in the race you're to run. No earthly event or test will ever dismiss us from the responsibility we carry toward our race or will diminish the interest our heavenly audience has in seeing us finish our race.

> **HEBREWS 12:1 & 2**
> **1 Wherefore seeing we also are compassed about with so great a cloud of witnesses, let us lay aside every weight, and the sin which doth so**

> easily beset us, and let us run with patience the race that is set before us,
> 2 Looking unto Jesus the author and finisher of our faith....

If we're to finish our race, we must lay aside every weight and sin that would slow and hinder us in our race. Depression, grief, and sorrow are all weights that would serve to hinder us in our running – they must be laid aside, and we must refuse to try to carry them with us in our race. Anything that won't accelerate your pace must be laid aside.

## Finish With Joy

Paul tells us how God revealed to him that he would face great persecutions once he arrived in Jerusalem. Although he knew difficulties were ahead, he still continued his race, never slowing his pace.

> **ACTS 20:22-24**
> 22 And now, behold, I go bound in the spirit unto Jerusalem, not knowing the things that shall befall me there:
> 23 Save that the Holy Ghost witnesseth in every city, saying that bonds and afflictions abide me.
> 24 But NONE OF THESE THINGS MOVE ME, neither count I my life dear unto myself, so that I might FINISH MY COURSE WITH JOY, and the ministry, which I have received of the Lord Jesus, to testify the gospel of the grace of God.

No opposition moved him from finishing his course with joy. Staying in joy helped him finish.

**The Joy Of The Lord Is Your Strength**

In Nehemiah 8:10, we're instructed, *"...neither be ye sorry* (Amplified – be not grieved and depressed)*; for the joy of the Lord is your strength."*

How does the Lord strengthen us? He has put His joy in us. As we yield to and draw out the joy that He has put in us, strength flows, for joy produces strength. To leave joy is to leave strength.

Since the joy of the Lord is my strength, I can't afford to step out of joy for even one moment, for if I do, I lose my strength, and I need His strength to run my race.

**Don't Be Grieved Or Depressed**

We're warned in Nehemiah to not be grieved or depressed, because those things steal our joy, and then we lose our strength when joy is lost.

Joy is a fruit of the spirit that God put in you at the new birth (Galatians 5:22), but although it's in you, you have to yield to and draw on that joy. How do you do that? Paul told Timothy to STIR UP the gift of God that was in him (2 Tim. 1:6). Everything that God puts in you has to be stirred up for it to flow, and you're the one who has to stir it up.

How do you stir up the joy that's in you when you feel like weeping and may be feeling grief and sorrow? Paul tells you how to stir up and draw out the joy that's in you in Philippians 4:4, *"Rejoice in the Lord always; and again I say, Rejoice."*

As you make the choice to rejoice, especially when you don't feel like it, joy will begin to flow, and when it does, you'll be strengthened. Your faith will be strengthened. Your body will be strengthened. Your whole being will be strengthened. But it is a choice you must make.

How long do you need to rejoice? Until the joy is overflowing!

## Count It All Joy

James knew this same truth when he instructed us to, *"...count it all joy when ye fall into divers temptations"* (James 1:2). Every situation doesn't offer you joy, that's why you have to count it joy and stir up joy in the face of that situation. You can rejoice in tests and difficulties because the Greater One is in you, and He will put you over. Nothing is greater than the Greater One in you! You can rejoice in the face of difficulty because you know that victory will be the outcome as you rejoice.

The exit road out of any difficulty, test, and trial is paved with rejoicing. Until you rejoice right in the midst of difficulty, you won't come out of the test. That's why James instructs us to count it all joy when we encounter difficulties. The sooner you rejoice, the sooner you'll exit that test.

As one minister stated, "When you pray, you lay hold of things, but when you praise, you win battles!"

## Put on Praise

Some may say, "I am so entrenched in and overcome by depression that it's even hard for me to function. What do I do?" Isaiah 61:3 talks about, *"...the garment of praise for the spirit of heaviness* (depression)."

A garment has to be put on, so it's up to us to put on the garment of praise that God has provided for us. As we do that, daily and faithfully, depression will fall off.

As you begin to praise the Lord, rejoicing in the victory that Jesus provided for you, strength will begin to flow.

Joy is the trump card that you are to play that will trump any opposition. No matter what the test or opposition, if you will begin to rejoice, you'll overcome every time!

Since the joy of the Lord is your strength, stay in the flow of joy every day through rejoicing. As you do, strength will flow and victory will be yours!

You have a race to run and to finish. It matters how you run, and it matters how you finish. Run in joy and finish in joy, for the grandstands of Heaven are watching!

*Chapter 10*

# A Husband to the Widow

One of the first things that came to me when I heard that Ed went to Heaven was that God is the Husband to the widow (Isaiah 54:4 & 5).

My husband was so good and generous toward me. If he knew that there was something I wanted, he made it his assignment to get it for me, no matter what it was. (Now, because I knew that he was that way toward me, I made sure that I never took advantage of that.)

I reminded God how good my husband had always been to me, and I knew that God, Who was now my Husband, wouldn't be outdone by Ed.

I knew that just because my husband had gone to Heaven, it didn't mean that I would have to live a "less-than" life; I knew that my Heavenly Husband would see to that.

If widows think that they have to live a "less-than" life, the enemy will take advantage of that kind of thinking and rob from them.

Yet, I knew that just because I was now a widow, that didn't dismiss me from having to exercise my faith. I still have to feed and release my faith, for God won't bypass His Word just because I'm a widow.

Hebrews 13:6 tells us that we are to *boldly* say, *"...The Lord is my helper...."* How does He help us? By putting His words in our mouths. As we speak His Word, then He is able to help us. But if we don't speak His Word, then He's unable to help us. He doesn't just help me because I'm a widow – He helps me because I speak His Word. When I speak His Word, then He fulfills it.

Matthew 8:17 says, *"That it might be fulfilled which was spoken...."* God can only fulfill what is spoken. The unspoken goes unfulfilled. Therefore, the more you speak, the more He will fulfill.

### God's Presence

Since my husband's homegoing, I have moved into a place of fellowship with God that I had never experienced until I became a widow.

God had told me that He had another home for me, and He showed me which home it was. In the process of purchasing that home, God's presence would manifest many times and stay tangible for hours. I had never experienced anything quite like this before. At those times, He would begin to converse with me about every detail of this home-buying process.

One day I said to Him, "I've never known this place of fellowship with You before, with You conversing so intimately with me about every detail of this new home."

He answered me, "If your husband were with you, these are the details you would intimately discuss with him. Since I am now your Husband, I am present to have those same discussions with you."

I saw in such a precious way how nothing of what I needed in life was lost to me. God's presence as a Husband to the widow makes all the difference for me.

Until I was a widow, I had never experienced this intimacy of fellowship with Him, for He was now to me that fellowship that my husband had previously been to me.

### Aloneness Vs. Loneliness

Not only are we redeemed from grief and sorrow, but we are redeemed from loneliness. Yes, naturally speaking, I find myself alone much more, but aloneness is not the same as loneliness. Although I'm often alone, I'm never lonely – I refuse to be.

God has never left me to be alone. I have my Father's constant companionship and fellowship. Any sense of loneliness is a torment of the enemy, and I resist it and won't receive it.

If a person begins to yield to self-pity or self-sympathy, they will certainly open the door to loneliness to come in and trouble them. But don't give any such place to the devil.

Your times of being alone can become your greatest times of fellowship and intimacy with your Heavenly Husband.

Value what He is now to you, and lay great emphasis upon it.

Yes, for those of you who are widows or widowers, this is a new season and a new chapter of your life. Although it's different than previous seasons, it's not a "less-than" season.

God's Word, along with His fellowship, strength, peace, joy, and plan are still yours! The path of the righteous grows brighter and brighter, not duller and dimmer (Proverbs 4:18).

God's plan for your life is still in place. There is still much for you to do, and much fruit for you to bear.

Walk in the light of the Word. Rejoice in Him every day of your life. Lay hold of all the richness that He has made yours. Keep pressing and reaching forward. And choose to live days of Heaven on the earth!

# Prayer of Salvation

Dear Heavenly Father:

I come to You in the Name of Jesus. Your Word says, *"...him that cometh to me I will in no wise cast out"* (John 6:37). So I know You won't cast me out, but You will take me in, and I thank You for it.

You said in Your Word, *"...If thou shalt confess with thy mouth the Lord Jesus, and shalt believe in thine heart that God hath raised him from the dead, thou shalt be saved. For whosoever shall call upon the name of the Lord shall be saved"* (Rom. 10:9 & 13).

I believe in my heart that Jesus Christ is the Son of God. I believe Jesus died for my sins and was raised from the dead so I can be in right-standing with God. I am calling upon His Name, the Name of Jesus, so I know, Father, that You save me now.

Your Word says, *"...with the heart man believeth unto righteousness; and with the mouth confession is made unto salvation"* (Rom. 10:10). I do believe with my heart, and I confess Jesus now as my Lord. Therefore, I am saved! Thank You, Father.

Please write us and let us know that you have just been born again. When you write, ask to receive our salvation booklets.

To contact us, please email us at
dm@dufresneministries.org
or write to:
Dufresne Ministries
P.O. Box 1010
Murrieta, CA 92564

# How to be Filled with the Holy Spirit

Acts 2:38 reads, *"...Repent, and be baptized every one of you in the name of Jesus Christ for the remission of sins, and ye shall receive the GIFT of the Holy Ghost."* The Holy Ghost is a gift that belongs to each one of God's people. Jesus is the gift God gave the whole world, but the Holy Spirit is a gift that belongs only to God's people.

Jesus told His disciples, *"But ye shall receive POWER, after that the Holy Ghost is come upon you: and ye shall be witnesses unto me..."* (Acts 1:8). When you're baptized with the Holy Spirit, you receive supernatural power that enables you to live victoriously.

## Indwelling vs. Infilling

When you're born again, you receive the indwelling of the Person of the Holy Spirit. Romans 8:16 tells us, *"The Spirit itself* (Himself) *beareth witness with our spirit, that we are the children of God."* When you're born again, you know it because the Spirit bears witness with your own spirit that you are a child of God; He confirms it to you. He's able to bear witness with your spirit because He's in you; you are *indwelt* by the Spirit of God.

But the Word of God speaks of another experience subsequent to the new birth that belongs to every believer, and that is to be baptized with the Holy Spirit, or to receive the *infilling* of the Holy Spirit.

God wants you to be full and overflowing with the Spirit. Being filled with the Spirit is likened to being full of water. Just because you had one drink of water doesn't mean you're full of water. At the new birth, you received the indwelling of the Spirit – a drink of water. But now God wants you to be filled to overflowing – be filled with His Spirit, baptized with the Holy Ghost.

> **ACTS 2:1-4**
> **1 And when the day of Pentecost was fully come, they were all with one accord in one place.**
> **2 And suddenly there came a sound from heaven as of a rushing mighty wind, and it filled all the house where they were sitting.**
> **3 And there appeared unto them cloven tongues like as of fire, and it sat upon each of them.**
> **4 And they were all FILLED with the Holy Ghost, and BEGAN TO SPEAK WITH OTHER TONGUES, as the Spirit gave them utterance.**

When these disciples were filled with the Holy Ghost, they began to speak with other tongues as the Spirit gave them utterance; they spoke in a language unknown to them. Today, when a believer is filled with the Holy Ghost, they will speak with other tongues too. These are not words that come from the mind of man, but they are words given by the Holy Spirit; these words float up from their spirit within, and the person then speaks those out.

What is the benefit of being filled with the Holy Ghost with the evidence of speaking in other tongues? First Corinthians 14:2 reads, *"For he that speaketh in an unknown tongue speaketh not unto men, but unto God...."* When you're speaking in other tongues, you're speaking to God – it is a divine means of communicating with your Heavenly Father. This is one of many great benefits.

> **MATTHEW 7:7-11**
> **7 Ask, and it shall be given you...**
> **8 FOR EVERY ONE THAT ASKETH RECEIVETH...**
> **9 ...what man is there of you, whom if his son ask bread, will he give him a stone?**
> **10 Or if he ask a fish, will he give him a serpent?**
> **11 If ye then, being evil, know how to give good gifts unto your children, HOW MUCH MORE SHALL YOUR FATHER WHICH IS IN HEAVEN GIVE GOOD THINGS TO THEM THAT ASK HIM?**

In this passage, Jesus is saying that when you ask God for something, you shall receive it! Believe that He will give you that which you ask for. When you ask God for something good, He won't give you something that will harm you; He will give you the good thing you ask for. The baptism of the Holy Spirit is a good gift, and when you ask God to fill you with the Holy Spirit, you won't receive a wrong spirit; you will receive this good gift, the gift of the Holy Spirit.

Once you receive the gift of the Holy Ghost, you can yield to this gift any time, speaking in other tongues as often as you choose; you don't have to wait for God to move on you. The more you speak in other tongues, the more you will benefit from this gift. By continuing to speak in other tongues on a daily basis, you will be able to maintain a Spirit-filled life; you will live full of the Spirit.

The more you take time to speak in other tongues, the deeper you'll move into the things of God.

(For more teaching on being filled with the Holy Spirit, I recommend the mini-book, *Why Tongues?* by Kenneth E. Hagin.)

# Prayer to Receive the Holy Spirit

*"Father, I see that the gift of the Holy Spirit belongs to Your children. So, I come to You to receive this gift. I received my salvation by faith, so I receive the gift of the Holy Spirit by faith. I believe I receive the Holy Spirit now! Since I'm filled with the Holy Spirit now, I expect to speak in other tongues as the Spirit gives me utterance, just like those in Acts 2 on the Day of Pentecost. Thank You for filling me with the Holy Ghost."*

Now, words that the Spirit of God gives you will float up from your spirit. You are the one who must open your mouth and speak those words out. The words will not come to your mind, but they will float up from your spirit. Speak those out freely.